Mastering Remote Work: Strategies for Success in the Digital Age

Copyright© 2024 Anthony Davies & Mobolaji Wale-Awe

All rights reserved

Table of Contents

Introduction: The Rise of Remote Work

- The Evolution of Work
- Benefits of Remote Work
- Challenges and Opportunities

Setting Up for Success

- Creating an Optimal Workspace
- Essential Tools and Technologies
- Ergonomics and Health Considerations

Mastering Productivity

- Time Management Techniques
- Setting Goals and Priorities
- Overcoming Procrastination

Effective Communication

- Choosing the Right Communication Tools
- Building Strong Virtual Teams
- Managing Meetings and Collaboration

Work-Life Balance

- Setting Boundaries Between Work and Personal Life
- Strategies for Maintaining Mental Health
- Tips for Staying Motivated

Security and Privacy

- Protecting Sensitive Information
- Best Practices for Cybersecurity
- Tools for Secure Communication

Building a Remote Work Culture

- Creating a Sense of Community
- Encouraging Team Engagement
- Fostering Trust and Accountability

Case Studies of Successful Remote Teams

- Insights from Leading Remote Companies
- Lessons Learned and Best Practices
- Interviews with Remote Work Experts

The Future of Remote Work

- Trends to Watch
- Preparing for a Hybrid Work Environment
- Predictions and Opportunities

Conclusion: Embracing the Remote Work Revolution

- Recap of Key Strategies
- Encouragement for Continued Growth
- Resources for Further Learning

Chapter 1: Introduction: The Rise of Remote Work

The New Age of Work

In a world that's constantly evolving, the concept of work has undergone a significant transformation. Gone are the days when a typical workday was confined within the four walls of an office. The rise of remote work has reshaped our understanding of productivity, flexibility, and work-life balance. As we step into this new era, it's essential to understand the journey that has brought us here, the benefits and challenges that come with remote work, and the opportunities it presents for the future.

The Evolution of Work

Remote work, once a rare privilege, has now become a global phenomenon. The seeds of this transformation were sown decades ago with the advent of the internet, but it wasn't until the early 21st century that remote work started to gain significant traction. Early adopters, primarily in the tech industry, began to explore the possibilities of working from home, driven by the need for flexibility and the desire to attract top talent regardless of geographical boundaries.

The turning point came with advancements in technology. High-speed internet, cloud computing, and collaborative tools like Slack, Zoom, and Trello made it possible for teams to stay connected and productive from anywhere in the world. These innovations paved the way for a shift in mindset—one that recognized that work is not a place you go to, but something you do.

The COVID-19 pandemic served as a catalyst for the remote work revolution. As offices closed and social distancing became the norm, businesses were forced to adapt quickly. What was initially a temporary solution soon proved to be a viable long-term strategy. Employees discovered the perks of working from home, and employers noted sustained or even increased productivity levels.

Benefits of Remote Work

Remote work offers a plethora of benefits, making it an attractive option for both employees and employers.

For Employees:

1. **Flexibility:** Remote work allows employees to create a schedule that fits their personal and professional lives. This flexibility can lead to improved job satisfaction and reduced stress levels.
2. **Time Savings:** Without the daily commute, employees can save valuable time and reduce the stress associated with traveling to and from work. This extra time can be used for personal activities, hobbies, or spending time with family.
3. **Increased Productivity:** Many employees find that they are more productive when working from home. With fewer distractions and the ability to create a personalized work environment, tasks can be completed more efficiently.
4. **Cost Savings:** Remote work can lead to significant savings on expenses such as commuting, work attire, and daily meals.

For Employers:

1. **Access to a Global Talent Pool:** Remote work removes geographical limitations, allowing employers to hire the best talent from around the world. This diversity can lead to innovative ideas and perspectives.

2. **Reduced Overhead Costs:** With fewer employees in the office, companies can save on rent, utilities, and other operational expenses.
3. **Increased Employee Retention:** Offering remote work options can improve employee satisfaction and loyalty, leading to higher retention rates and reduced turnover costs.
4. **Sustainability:** Remote work can contribute to environmental sustainability by reducing the need for commuting, thus lowering carbon footprints.

Challenges and Opportunities

While the benefits of remote work are significant, it also presents a unique set of challenges.

Challenges:

1. **Communication Barriers:** Without face-to-face interactions, communication can become more challenging. Misunderstandings and delays can occur if communication is not managed effectively.
2. **Isolation and Loneliness:** Working remotely can lead to feelings of isolation, especially for those who thrive on social interactions. It's crucial to find ways to stay connected with colleagues and maintain a sense of community.
3. **Work-Life Balance:** The line between work and personal life can blur when working from home. It's important to set boundaries to ensure a healthy work-life balance.
4. **Technology Issues:** Reliable internet access and up-to-date technology are essential for remote work. Technical difficulties can disrupt productivity and cause frustration.

Opportunities:

1. **Innovation in Collaboration Tools:** The demand for effective remote collaboration tools is driving innovation in this space. New technologies and platforms are constantly emerging to improve the remote work experience.
2. **Flexible Work Policies:** Companies are rethinking their work policies to offer more flexible options, including hybrid models that combine remote and in-office work. This flexibility can attract top talent and improve employee satisfaction.
3. **Global Collaboration:** Remote work enables teams from different parts of the world to collaborate seamlessly. This global perspective can lead to innovative solutions and a more inclusive work environment.
4. **Focus on Results:** With remote work, the emphasis shifts from hours worked to results achieved. This performance-based approach can lead to higher productivity and more motivated employees.

Embracing the Remote Work Revolution

As we navigate the complexities of remote work, it's clear that this is more than just a passing trend—it's a fundamental shift in how we approach our careers and daily routines. By understanding the evolution of work, recognizing the benefits and challenges, and seizing the opportunities, we can fully embrace the remote work revolution.

In the following chapters, we will delve deeper into the strategies and tools needed to succeed in a remote work environment. From setting up an optimal workspace to mastering productivity, effective communication, and maintaining a healthy work-life balance, this book will equip you with the knowledge and skills to thrive in the digital age.

Stay tuned as we embark on this journey to mastering remote work, transforming challenges into opportunities, and redefining success in the modern workplace.

Chapter 2: Setting Up for Success

Laying the Foundation for Remote Work Excellence

Transitioning to remote work isn't just about changing your location; it's about setting up an environment that fosters productivity, creativity, and well-being. The foundation you lay now will significantly impact your remote work experience. This chapter delves into the essentials of creating an optimal workspace, selecting the right tools and technologies, and prioritizing ergonomics and health to ensure long-term success.

Creating an Optimal Workspace

Your workspace is more than just a desk and a chair—it's the epicenter of your productivity and focus. Here are some key considerations to ensure your workspace supports your remote work journey:

1. Choose the Right Location:

- **Quiet and Private:** Select a space that minimizes interruptions. If possible, choose a room with a door to signal to others when you are working.
- **Natural Light:** Position your workspace near a window to benefit from natural light, which can boost your mood and energy levels.
- **Consistent Setup:** Avoid working from your bed or couch. Consistently using a designated workspace helps create a mental distinction between work and leisure.

2. Organize Your Space:

- **Declutter:** A clutter-free environment reduces stress and distractions. Keep only essential items on your desk and store others neatly.
- **Personal Touch:** Add personal items like photos, plants, or artwork to make your space inviting and comfortable.
- **Accessibility:** Arrange your workspace so that frequently used items are within easy reach, reducing unnecessary movements and disruptions.

3. Optimize Your Desk Setup:

- **Monitor Height:** Ensure your monitor is at eye level to prevent neck strain. Use a monitor stand or a stack of books if needed.
- **Keyboard and Mouse Position:** Your keyboard and mouse should be at a comfortable height to avoid wrist strain. Consider using an ergonomic keyboard and mouse for added comfort.
- **Comfortable Seating:** Invest in a quality chair that provides good lumbar support. Your feet should rest flat on the floor, and your knees should be at a 90-degree angle.

Essential Tools and Technologies

Equipping yourself with the right tools can significantly enhance your remote work experience. Here are the must-have tools and technologies for remote workers:

1. Reliable Internet Connection:

- **High-Speed Internet:** A stable, high-speed internet connection is crucial for seamless communication and efficient work. Consider a backup option, such as a mobile hotspot, in case of connectivity issues.

2. Communication Tools:

- **Video Conferencing:** Tools like Zoom, Microsoft Teams, and Google Meet facilitate virtual meetings and face-to-face interactions.
- **Instant Messaging:** Slack, Microsoft Teams, and WhatsApp are excellent for quick, real-time communication with colleagues.

3. Project Management Software:

- **Task Management:** Tools like Trello, Asana, and Monday.com help you organize tasks, set deadlines, and collaborate with team members.
- **Document Sharing:** Google Drive, Dropbox, and OneDrive allow for easy sharing and collaboration on documents and files.

4. Productivity Apps:

- **Time Tracking:** Apps like Toggl, Clockify, and RescueTime help you track time spent on tasks and identify areas for improvement.

- **Focus Tools:** Tools like Focus@Will, Freedom, and Pomodoro timers can help you stay focused and manage your time effectively.

5. Security Tools:

- **VPN:** A Virtual Private Network (VPN) ensures secure internet connections, especially when using public Wi-Fi.
- **Password Managers:** Tools like LastPass, 1Password, and Dashlane securely store and manage your passwords.

Ergonomics and Health Considerations

Maintaining good health is crucial for sustaining long-term productivity and well-being. Here are some tips to ensure your workspace supports your physical and mental health:

1. Ergonomic Furniture:

- **Ergonomic Chair:** A chair with adjustable height, lumbar support, and armrests can prevent back pain and promote good posture.
- **Standing Desk:** Consider a standing desk or a desk converter to alternate between sitting and standing throughout the day.

2. Good Posture:

- **Monitor at Eye Level:** Keep your monitor at eye level to avoid straining your neck.
- **Neutral Wrist Position:** Your wrists should be in a neutral position, not bent up or down, to prevent strain.
- **Foot Position:** Your feet should be flat on the floor or on a footrest.

3. Regular Breaks:

- **The 20-20-20 Rule:** Every 20 minutes, look at something 20 feet away for at least 20 seconds to reduce eye strain.
- **Stretching:** Incorporate regular stretching or movement breaks to relieve muscle tension and improve circulation.

- **Physical Activity:** Aim for at least 30 minutes of physical activity daily. This could be a walk, workout, or simple stretching exercises.

4. **Mental Health:**

    - **Set Boundaries:** Establish clear boundaries between work and personal life to avoid burnout. Create a routine that signals the start and end of your workday.
    - **Social Interaction:** Stay connected with colleagues through virtual coffee breaks, team-building activities, and casual chats.
    - **Mindfulness Practices:** Incorporate mindfulness techniques, such as meditation or deep breathing exercises, to manage stress and maintain focus.

Building Your Remote Work Arsenal

Setting up for remote work success requires thoughtful planning and investment in the right tools and practices. By creating an optimal workspace, equipping yourself with essential tools and technologies, and prioritizing ergonomics and health, you can lay a strong foundation for a productive and fulfilling remote work experience.

Chapter 3: Mastering Productivity

Unlocking the Secrets of Peak Performance

Remote work offers unparalleled flexibility, but it also requires a high level of self-discipline and productivity. Without the structure of a traditional office environment, staying focused and managing your time effectively can be challenging. This chapter delves into the art of mastering productivity, offering proven strategies and practical tips to help you achieve peak performance in your remote work journey.

Time Management Techniques

Time management is the cornerstone of productivity. Effective time management allows you to accomplish more in less time, reduce stress, and achieve a better work-life balance. Here are some essential techniques to help you manage your time efficiently:

1. The Pomodoro Technique:

- **Work in Intervals:** Break your work into 25-minute intervals (Pomodoros) followed by a 5-minute break. After four Pomodoros, take a longer break of 15-30 minutes.
- **Maintain Focus:** This technique helps you maintain focus and avoid burnout by working in short, concentrated bursts.
- **Track Progress:** Use a timer or a Pomodoro app to keep track of your intervals and monitor your productivity.

2. Time Blocking:

- **Schedule Tasks:** Allocate specific blocks of time for different tasks throughout your day. For example, dedicate mornings to high-priority tasks and afternoons to meetings or administrative work.

- **Avoid Multitasking:** Focus on one task during each block of time to improve concentration and efficiency.
- **Review and Adjust:** At the end of each day, review your schedule and make adjustments as needed for the following day.

3. The Eisenhower Matrix:

- **Prioritize Tasks:** Categorize tasks into four quadrants based on their urgency and importance:
    - **Urgent and Important:** Do these tasks immediately.
    - **Important but Not Urgent:** Schedule these tasks for later.
    - **Urgent but Not Important:** Delegate these tasks if possible.
    - **Not Urgent and Not Important:** Eliminate or minimize these tasks.
- **Focus on What Matters:** This matrix helps you prioritize tasks that contribute to your long-term goals and reduce time spent on less important activities.

4. The Two-Minute Rule:

- **Act Quickly:** If a task takes less than two minutes to complete, do it immediately. This prevents small tasks from piling up and becoming overwhelming.
- **Minimize Procrastination:** The two-minute rule helps you tackle small tasks efficiently, keeping your to-do list manageable.

Setting Goals and Priorities

Setting clear goals and priorities is essential for maintaining focus and direction in your remote work. Goals give you a sense of purpose, while priorities help you allocate your time and resources effectively. Here's how to set and achieve your goals:

1. SMART Goals:

- **Specific:** Clearly define your goals with specific details. Instead of "increase productivity," aim for "complete three major projects this month."
- **Measurable:** Establish criteria to measure your progress. For example, track the number of tasks completed or the time spent on each project.
- **Achievable:** Set realistic and attainable goals. Ensure you have the resources and capabilities to achieve them.
- **Relevant:** Align your goals with your long-term objectives and values. Ensure they contribute to your overall mission.
- **Time-bound:** Set a deadline for each goal to create a sense of urgency and keep yourself accountable.

2. Daily and Weekly Planning:

- **Daily To-Do Lists:** Start each day with a list of tasks you aim to complete. Prioritize them based on importance and deadlines.
- **Weekly Reviews:** At the end of each week, review your progress, celebrate achievements, and plan for the upcoming week.

3. The 80/20 Rule (Pareto Principle):

- **Identify Key Tasks:** Focus on the 20% of tasks that yield 80% of the results. Prioritize these high-impact tasks to maximize your productivity.
- **Eliminate Low-Value Activities:** Identify and minimize activities that contribute little to your goals. Delegate or

eliminate these tasks to free up time for more important work.

Overcoming Procrastination

Procrastination is a common challenge for remote workers. Without the external pressure of an office environment, it's easy to put off tasks and fall into the trap of procrastination. Here are some strategies to help you overcome procrastination:

1. Break Tasks into Smaller Steps:

- **Manageable Chunks:** Divide large tasks into smaller, more manageable steps. This makes the task less daunting and easier to start.
- **Progress Tracking:** Track your progress with each small step completed, providing a sense of accomplishment and motivation to continue.

2. Set Deadlines:

- **Create Urgency:** Set clear deadlines for each task to create a sense of urgency and avoid endless postponement.
- **Use External Accountability:** Share your deadlines with a colleague, friend, or mentor who can help keep you accountable.

3. Eliminate Distractions:

- **Identify Triggers:** Recognize the activities or environments that trigger procrastination. Minimize these distractions during work hours.
- **Focus Tools:** Use apps and tools like website blockers, noise-canceling headphones, and focus playlists to create a distraction-free work environment.

4. **Practice Self-Compassion:**

   - **Acknowledge Feelings:** Understand that procrastination is a common experience. Be kind to yourself and avoid self-criticism.
   - **Reward Progress:** Celebrate small victories and reward yourself for completing tasks, reinforcing positive behavior and motivation.

Tools for Enhancing Productivity

Leveraging the right tools can significantly boost your productivity and streamline your remote work processes. Here are some essential productivity tools:

1. **Task Management Apps:**

   - **Trello:** Visualize your tasks with boards, lists, and cards. Collaborate with team members and track progress.
   - **Asana:** Manage tasks, projects, and workflows with customizable templates and integrations.
   - **Todoist:** Create simple to-do lists, set priorities, and track your progress with a user-friendly interface.

2. **Time Tracking Apps:**

   - **Toggl:** Track time spent on tasks and projects. Generate detailed reports to analyze your productivity.
   - **Clockify:** A free time tracker and timesheet app for individuals and teams. Track work hours and monitor productivity.
   - **RescueTime:** Monitor your computer usage, identify time-wasting activities, and set goals to improve focus.

3. Focus and Distraction Management Tools:

- **Focus@Will:** Music designed to improve focus and concentration, helping you stay productive.
- **Freedom:** Block distracting websites and apps to create a distraction-free work environment.
- **Forest:** Stay focused by planting virtual trees. The longer you stay on task, the more your forest grows.

4. Collaboration Tools:

- **Slack:** Real-time messaging, file sharing, and collaboration for remote teams.
- **Microsoft Teams:** Integrates with Office 365 for seamless communication, meetings, and collaboration.
- **Google Workspace:** Collaborative tools like Google Docs, Sheets, and Drive for real-time teamwork.

Achieving Mastery in Remote Work Productivity

Mastering productivity in a remote work environment requires a combination of effective time management, goal setting, and overcoming procrastination. By implementing these strategies and leveraging the right tools, you can achieve peak performance and maintain a healthy work-life balance.

Chapter 4: Communication and Collaboration

The Backbone of Remote Work Success

Effective communication and collaboration are the bedrock of any successful remote work environment. While working from different locations offers flexibility, it also presents unique challenges in maintaining clear and consistent communication. This chapter delves into the strategies, tools, and best practices that ensure seamless interaction and collaboration among remote teams, fostering a productive and cohesive work culture.

The Importance of Clear Communication

Clear communication is crucial for remote teams to stay aligned, meet deadlines, and achieve their goals. Without the ability to pop by a colleague's desk or have impromptu meetings, remote workers must rely on virtual communication methods. Here's why clarity in communication is essential:

1. Reduces Misunderstandings:

- **Explicit Instructions:** Clear, detailed instructions help prevent misinterpretations and ensure that everyone understands their tasks and responsibilities.
- **Consistency:** Regular, consistent communication keeps all team members on the same page, reducing the likelihood of errors.

2. Builds Trust:

- **Transparency:** Open and honest communication fosters trust among team members. It creates a sense of accountability and reliability.
- **Relationship Building:** Regular check-ins and updates help build relationships and camaraderie, even when working remotely.

3. Enhances Productivity:

- **Quick Resolutions:** Clear communication channels enable quick problem-solving and decision-making, boosting overall productivity.
- **Focused Work:** With clear goals and expectations, team members can focus on their tasks without second-guessing.

Essential Communication Tools

Choosing the right tools is fundamental to facilitating effective communication and collaboration in a remote work environment. Here are some essential tools and their best use cases:

1. Instant Messaging:

- **Slack:** Ideal for real-time messaging, file sharing, and creating channels for specific teams or projects.
- **Microsoft Teams:** Integrates with Office 365, offering chat, video meetings, and file collaboration in one platform.
- **Discord:** Originally designed for gamers, now also used by remote teams for voice, video, and text communication.

2. Video Conferencing:

- **Zoom:** Popular for its ease of use, reliable performance, and features like breakout rooms and screen sharing.
- **Google Meet:** Part of Google Workspace, offering seamless integration with other Google tools and services.
- **Skype:** Long-standing video conferencing tool with chat and file-sharing capabilities.

3. Project Management:

- **Trello:** Visual task management with boards, lists, and cards to organize projects and track progress.
- **Asana:** Comprehensive project management tool for planning, tracking, and managing team projects and tasks.
- **Monday.com:** Customizable workflows and project tracking with visual timelines and automation features.

4. Document Collaboration:

- **Google Workspace:** Includes Google Docs, Sheets, and Slides for real-time collaboration and sharing.
- **Microsoft 365:** Offers collaborative tools like Word, Excel, and PowerPoint with cloud storage and sharing.
- **Dropbox Paper:** A collaborative document editing tool integrated with Dropbox for easy file management.

Best Practices for Effective Communication

To maximize the effectiveness of your communication efforts, consider implementing these best practices:

1. Establish Clear Guidelines:

- **Communication Channels:** Define which tools to use for different types of communication (e.g., Slack for quick messages, Zoom for meetings).
- **Response Times:** Set expectations for response times to ensure timely communication without overburdening team members.

2. Regular Check-Ins:

- **Daily Stand-Ups:** Brief daily meetings where team members share updates on their tasks, challenges, and plans for the day.
- **Weekly Meetings:** Longer meetings to discuss progress, upcoming tasks, and any issues that need addressing.
- **One-on-One Meetings:** Regular check-ins between managers and team members to discuss individual performance and provide support.

3. Use Asynchronous Communication:

- **Documentation:** Encourage thorough documentation of processes, decisions, and project updates. Tools like Confluence or Notion are excellent for this purpose.
- **Flexibility:** Allow team members to work and respond at their own pace, accommodating different time zones and schedules.

4. Foster a Culture of Openness:

- **Encourage Feedback:** Create an environment where team members feel comfortable sharing their ideas, feedback, and concerns.
- **Transparency:** Share company goals, progress, and challenges openly to keep everyone informed and engaged.

Collaboration Strategies for Remote Teams

Effective collaboration is more than just communication; it's about working together towards common goals. Here are strategies to enhance collaboration among remote teams:

1. Define Roles and Responsibilities:

- **Clarity:** Clearly define each team member's role and responsibilities to avoid overlap and confusion.
- **Accountability:** Establish accountability by assigning ownership of tasks and projects.

2. Leverage Collaborative Tools:

- **Shared Platforms:** Use shared platforms like Google Drive, Dropbox, or OneDrive for easy access to files and collaborative editing.
- **Integrated Workflows:** Integrate tools like Slack, Trello, and Asana to streamline workflows and ensure seamless collaboration.

3. Create a Virtual Watercooler:

- **Informal Channels:** Create informal communication channels (e.g., a #watercooler channel on Slack) for casual conversations and team bonding.
- **Virtual Social Events:** Organize virtual social events like coffee breaks, game nights, or happy hours to build team rapport.

4. Encourage Cross-Functional Collaboration:

- **Interdisciplinary Teams:** Form teams with members from different departments or disciplines to bring diverse perspectives to projects.
- **Knowledge Sharing:** Promote knowledge sharing through regular presentations, workshops, or internal newsletters.

Overcoming Remote Communication Challenges

Remote work comes with its own set of communication challenges. Here's how to address some common issues:

1. Time Zone Differences:

- **Flexible Scheduling:** Allow flexible working hours to accommodate different time zones.
- **Overlap Hours:** Identify overlapping hours where team members in different time zones can collaborate in real-time.

2. Lack of Non-Verbal Cues:

- **Use Video:** Whenever possible, use video calls instead of audio-only calls to capture non-verbal cues and build stronger connections.

- **Emojis and GIFs:** Encourage the use of emojis and GIFs in chat messages to convey tone and emotion.

3. **Information Overload:**

    - **Prioritize Communication:** Focus on essential communication and avoid overwhelming team members with unnecessary information.
    - **Structured Updates:** Use structured updates and summaries to keep communication concise and relevant.

4. **Building Trust:**

    - **Consistent Communication:** Maintain regular and consistent communication to build trust and transparency.
    - **Recognition and Appreciation:** Regularly recognize and appreciate team members' efforts to foster a positive and supportive environment.

Elevating Your Remote Work Collaboration

Mastering communication and collaboration is crucial for remote work success. By implementing the right tools, best practices, and strategies, you can overcome the challenges of remote work and create a cohesive, productive, and engaged team.

In the following chapters, we will explore the importance of maintaining a work-life balance, strategies for continuous learning and growth, and tips for creating a thriving remote work culture.

Chapter 5: Maintaining Work-Life Balance

Finding Harmony in the Remote Work Lifestyle

One of the greatest benefits of remote work is the flexibility it offers. However, with this flexibility comes the challenge of maintaining a healthy work-life balance. Without the clear boundaries of a traditional office, work can easily spill into personal time, leading to burnout and stress. This chapter explores strategies and practices to help you maintain a harmonious balance between your professional and personal life, ensuring both productivity and well-being.

Understanding the Importance of Work-Life Balance

Work-life balance is about creating a healthy equilibrium between your work responsibilities and personal life. It involves managing your time and energy effectively to ensure that neither your work nor personal life suffers. Here's why maintaining a good work-life balance is essential:

1. Enhances Well-Being:

- **Mental Health:** Proper work-life balance reduces stress and anxiety, contributing to better mental health.
- **Physical Health:** Adequate rest and personal time promote physical well-being and reduce the risk of burnout.

2. Increases Productivity:

- **Focused Work:** When you have a balanced life, you can focus better on your work during designated hours, leading to higher productivity.
- **Energy Levels:** Regular breaks and personal time help recharge your energy, making you more efficient.

3. Improves Relationships:

- **Personal Connections:** Spending quality time with family and friends strengthens your relationships.
- **Work Relationships:** A balanced life leads to better mood and interactions, improving relationships with colleagues and clients.

Strategies for Maintaining Work-Life Balance

Achieving a healthy work-life balance requires intentional effort and effective strategies. Here are some proven methods to help you maintain this balance:

1. Set Clear Boundaries:

- **Dedicated Workspace:** Create a designated workspace separate from your living areas to establish a physical boundary between work and personal life.
- **Work Hours:** Define your work hours and stick to them. Communicate these hours to your team and clients to set expectations.

2. Create a Daily Routine:

- **Consistent Schedule:** Establish a daily routine that includes work hours, breaks, and personal activities.

Consistency helps create a sense of normalcy and balance.
- **Morning Ritual:** Start your day with a morning ritual, such as exercise, meditation, or reading, to set a positive tone for the day.

3. Prioritize Self-Care:

- **Physical Health:** Incorporate regular exercise, a healthy diet, and adequate sleep into your daily routine.
- **Mental Health:** Practice mindfulness, meditation, or other stress-reducing activities to maintain mental well-being.
- **Hobbies and Interests:** Engage in hobbies and activities that you enjoy to unwind and recharge.

4. Use Technology Wisely:

- **Digital Detox:** Set boundaries for technology use, especially during personal time. Avoid checking work emails and messages outside of work hours.
- **Productivity Tools:** Use productivity tools and apps to manage your time effectively and reduce the likelihood of work spilling into personal time.

5. Take Regular Breaks:

- **Pomodoro Technique:** Work in intervals with short breaks in between. For example, work for 25 minutes, then take a 5-minute break.
- **Lunch Breaks:** Take a proper lunch break away from your workspace to refresh and recharge.

6. Plan Personal Time:

- **Schedule Activities:** Plan and schedule personal activities just as you would with work tasks. This ensures you make time for yourself and your loved ones.
- **Vacation and Days Off:** Take regular vacations and days off to disconnect from work and recharge.

Balancing Family and Work Life

Balancing family responsibilities with remote work can be particularly challenging. Here are some strategies to help you manage both effectively:

1. Communicate with Family:

- **Set Expectations:** Communicate your work schedule and boundaries with your family to ensure they understand when you need uninterrupted work time.
- **Involve Them:** Involve your family in creating a routine that works for everyone. This fosters understanding and cooperation.

2. Create Family Time:

- **Quality Time:** Dedicate specific times for family activities and ensure you are fully present during these times.
- **Flexible Scheduling:** If possible, create a flexible work schedule that allows you to attend important family events and activities.

3. Share Responsibilities:

- **Delegate Tasks:** Share household responsibilities with family members to ensure that you are not overwhelmed with both work and home duties.
- **Support System:** Build a support system of family, friends, or childcare services to help manage family responsibilities.

- **Dealing with Burnout**

Burnout is a state of physical, emotional, and mental exhaustion caused by prolonged stress and overwork. Recognizing the signs of burnout and taking steps to prevent it is crucial for maintaining work-life balance. Here's how to deal with burnout:

1. Recognize the Signs:

- **Exhaustion:** Persistent fatigue and lack of energy.
- **Detachment:** Feeling disconnected or indifferent towards work.
- **Decreased Performance:** Reduced productivity and difficulty concentrating.

2. Take Action:

- **Seek Support:** Talk to a manager, colleague, or mental health professional about your feelings and seek support.
- **Reduce Workload:** If possible, reduce your workload or delegate tasks to prevent further burnout.
- **Rest and Recharge:** Take time off to rest and recharge. Engage in activities that relax and rejuvenate you.

3. Implement Preventive Measures:

- **Set Realistic Goals:** Set achievable goals and avoid overcommitting yourself.

- **Practice Mindfulness:** Incorporate mindfulness practices, such as meditation or deep breathing, into your daily routine.
- **Maintain a Healthy Lifestyle:** Prioritize physical health through regular exercise, a balanced diet, and sufficient sleep.

Creating a Supportive Work Environment

A supportive work environment plays a significant role in maintaining work-life balance. Here's how organizations and managers can create such an environment for remote workers:

1. Promote Flexibility:

- **Flexible Hours:** Allow flexible working hours to accommodate personal and family responsibilities.
- **Remote Work Policies:** Develop remote work policies that prioritize work-life balance and employee well-being.

2. Encourage Regular Breaks:

- **Break Policies:** Encourage employees to take regular breaks and time off to recharge.
- **No-Meeting Days:** Implement no-meeting days to give employees uninterrupted time to focus on their work.

3. Foster a Positive Culture:

- **Supportive Leadership:** Leaders should model work-life balance and support employees in achieving it.
- **Recognition and Appreciation:** Regularly recognize and appreciate employees' efforts and contributions.

4. Provide Resources and Support:

- **Mental Health Resources:** Provide access to mental health resources, such as counseling services or wellness programs.
- **Work-Life Balance Programs:** Offer programs and initiatives that support work-life balance, such as flexible scheduling, childcare support, and wellness initiatives.

Thriving in a Balanced Remote Work Life

Maintaining work-life balance is crucial for long-term success and well-being in a remote work environment. By setting clear boundaries, prioritizing self-care, and leveraging supportive tools and strategies, you can achieve a harmonious balance between your professional and personal life.

Chapter 6: Continuous Learning and Growth

Embracing Lifelong Learning in the Remote Work Era

In today's fast-paced and ever-changing world, continuous learning and professional growth are not just advantageous but essential. Remote work offers the perfect environment to cultivate these habits, providing flexibility and access to a plethora of online resources. This chapter explores the importance of lifelong learning, strategies to integrate learning into your daily routine, and how to leverage online resources for personal and professional development.

The Importance of Lifelong Learning

Lifelong learning is the ongoing, voluntary, and self-motivated pursuit of knowledge. It encompasses a wide range of activities, from formal education to informal learning opportunities. Here's why embracing lifelong learning is crucial:

1. Adapting to Change:

- **Technological Advancements:** Rapid technological changes require continuous updating of skills and knowledge to stay relevant.
- **Industry Trends:** Staying informed about industry trends ensures you remain competitive and can adapt to new developments.

2. Enhancing Career Opportunities:

- **Skill Development:** Acquiring new skills opens up new career opportunities and paths for advancement.
- **Professional Growth:** Continuous learning enhances your expertise and makes you more valuable to current and potential employers.

3. Personal Fulfillment:

- **Intellectual Stimulation:** Learning new things keeps your mind active and engaged, providing a sense of accomplishment.
- **Passion Pursuit:** It allows you to explore areas of interest and develop hobbies, leading to a more fulfilling life.

Strategies for Integrating Learning into Your Routine

Balancing work and continuous learning requires intentional planning and effective strategies. Here are some ways to integrate learning into your daily routine:

1. **Set Clear Learning Goals:**

   - **Specific Objectives:** Define clear, specific learning goals that align with your career aspirations and personal interests.
   - **Short-Term and Long-Term Goals:** Set both short-term and long-term goals to maintain motivation and track progress.

2. **Create a Learning Schedule:**

   - **Dedicated Time:** Allocate specific times for learning activities in your daily or weekly schedule.
   - **Consistency:** Consistently dedicate time to learning, even if it's just a few minutes a day, to build a habit.

3. **Utilize Microlearning:**

   - **Short Sessions:** Engage in short, focused learning sessions to fit into your busy schedule.
   - **Bite-Sized Content:** Use microlearning platforms that offer bite-sized lessons and courses.

4. **Leverage Online Resources:**

   - **E-Learning Platforms:** Utilize platforms like Coursera, Udemy, LinkedIn Learning, and Khan Academy for a wide range of courses.
   - **Webinars and Workshops:** Participate in webinars, workshops, and virtual conferences to gain insights from industry experts.

5. **Join Professional Networks:**

- **Online Communities:** Join online communities and forums related to your field to share knowledge and learn from peers.
- **Professional Associations:** Become a member of professional associations to access exclusive resources and networking opportunities.

- **6. Read Regularly:**
- **Books and Articles:** Make a habit of reading books, articles, and journals related to your industry and interests.
- **Newsletters and Blogs:** Subscribe to industry newsletters and blogs to stay updated with the latest trends and insights.

Leveraging Online Resources for Learning

The internet offers a wealth of resources for continuous learning. Here's how to make the most of these resources:

1. E-Learning Platforms:

- **Coursera:** Offers courses from top universities and organizations, covering a wide range of subjects.
- **Udemy:** Provides a vast selection of courses on various topics, often with practical, hands-on lessons.
- **LinkedIn Learning:** Focuses on professional development courses, including business, technology, and creative skills.

2. Massive Open Online Courses (MOOCs):

- **edX:** Hosts courses from universities like Harvard and MIT, covering diverse fields.
- **FutureLearn:** Offers courses from universities and institutions worldwide, with a focus on social learning.

3. Certification Programs:

- **Industry Certifications:** Pursue certifications relevant to your field to validate your skills and enhance your resume.
- **Specialized Programs:** Enroll in specialized programs offered by industry leaders to gain advanced knowledge and skills.

4. Online Libraries and Repositories:

- **Google Scholar:** Access scholarly articles, research papers, and academic journals.
- **Project Gutenberg:** Offers a vast collection of free eBooks, including classics and historical texts.

5. Podcasts and Audiobooks:

- **Educational Podcasts:** Listen to podcasts on topics of interest during commutes or breaks.
- **Audiobooks:** Use platforms like Audible to listen to books while multitasking.

Creating a Personal Learning Plan

A personal learning plan helps you stay organized and focused on your learning journey. Here's how to create one:

1. Assess Your Current Skills:

- **Self-Evaluation:** Evaluate your current skills and identify areas for improvement.
- **Feedback:** Seek feedback from peers, mentors, or supervisors to gain insights into your strengths and weaknesses.

2. Define Learning Objectives:

- **SMART Goals:** Set Specific, Measurable, Achievable, Relevant, and Time-bound (SMART) goals for your learning.
- **Priority Areas:** Identify priority areas that align with your career goals and interests.

3. Identify Resources:

- **Courses and Programs:** Research and select courses, programs, or resources that align with your learning objectives.
- **Mentors and Networks:** Identify potential mentors or professional networks that can support your learning.

4. Create a Timeline:

- **Learning Schedule:** Develop a timeline for achieving your learning goals, with milestones to track progress.
- **Review and Adjust:** Regularly review your progress and adjust your plan as needed to stay on track.

5. Implement and Reflect:

- **Action Plan:** Implement your learning plan by engaging in selected courses, reading materials, and activities.
- **Reflection:** Reflect on your learning experiences and outcomes to identify areas for further improvement.

Encouraging a Learning Culture in Remote Teams

Creating a culture of continuous learning within remote teams enhances collective growth and innovation. Here's how to foster such a culture:

1. **Promote Learning Opportunities:**

   - **Learning Resources:** Provide access to learning resources and platforms for team members.
   - **Encouragement:** Encourage team members to pursue learning opportunities and share their experiences.

2. **Integrate Learning into Work:**

   - **Learning Projects:** Incorporate learning projects or assignments into work tasks to facilitate practical application.
   - **Collaboration:** Encourage collaboration and knowledge sharing among team members to enhance collective learning.

3. **Recognize and Reward Learning:**

   - **Recognition Programs:** Recognize and reward team members who actively engage in continuous learning.
   - **Professional Development:** Support professional development through training programs, workshops, and certifications.

4. **Provide Mentorship and Support:**

   - **Mentorship Programs:** Establish mentorship programs to support personal and professional growth.
   - **Feedback and Guidance:** Provide regular feedback and guidance to help team members achieve their learning goals.

Embracing a Growth Mindset

A growth mindset is the belief that abilities and intelligence can be developed through dedication and hard work. Embracing this mindset is key to continuous learning and growth. Here's how to cultivate a growth mindset:

1. Embrace Challenges:

- **Opportunity:** View challenges as opportunities to learn and grow.
- **Persistence:** Persist through obstacles and setbacks with a positive attitude.

2. Learn from Feedback:

- **Constructive Criticism:** Embrace constructive criticism as valuable feedback for improvement.
- **Self-Reflection:** Regularly reflect on your experiences and identify lessons learned.

3. Celebrate Effort:

- **Acknowledge Progress:** Celebrate your efforts and progress, not just the outcomes.
- **Motivation:** Stay motivated by recognizing the hard work and dedication you put into your learning journey.

Unlocking Your Potential Through Continuous Learning

Continuous learning and growth are vital for thriving in the remote work era. By setting clear goals, leveraging online resources, and fostering a culture of learning, you can unlock your potential and achieve personal and professional success.

Chapter 7: Building a Thriving Remote Work Culture

Cultivating a Positive and Productive Remote Work Environment

Creating a thriving remote work culture is crucial for the success of any organization that embraces remote work. A positive work culture fosters collaboration, enhances productivity, and improves employee satisfaction and retention. In this chapter, we'll explore the key elements of a successful remote work culture and provide practical strategies for cultivating a vibrant and cohesive virtual team environment.

The Importance of a Strong Remote Work Culture

A strong remote work culture is the foundation of an effective and harmonious remote team. Here's why it's essential:

1. Enhances Collaboration:

- **Team Cohesion:** A positive culture promotes teamwork and a sense of belonging, making remote employees feel connected to their colleagues.
- **Effective Communication:** Clear communication channels and a collaborative atmosphere enable team members to share ideas and work together efficiently.

2. Boosts Productivity:

- **Motivation:** A supportive work culture motivates employees to perform at their best and take ownership of their tasks.
- **Engagement:** Engaged employees are more likely to be productive and contribute to the organization's success.

3. Improves Employee Satisfaction and Retention:

- **Well-Being:** A culture that prioritizes employee well-being leads to higher job satisfaction and lower turnover rates.
- **Recognition:** Recognizing and valuing employees' contributions fosters loyalty and commitment.

Key Elements of a Thriving Remote Work Culture

Building a thriving remote work culture involves several key elements:

1. Clear Communication:

- **Transparent Communication:** Encourage open and honest communication to build trust and transparency.
- **Regular Updates:** Provide regular updates on company news, goals, and changes to keep everyone informed.

2. Trust and Autonomy:

- **Empowerment:** Trust your team members to manage their tasks and make decisions autonomously.
- **Accountability:** Hold employees accountable for their work while giving them the freedom to approach tasks in their own way.

3. Inclusivity and Diversity:

- **Diverse Teams:** Foster a diverse and inclusive work environment where different perspectives are valued.
- **Equitable Opportunities:** Ensure all team members have access to equal opportunities for growth and development.

4. Recognition and Appreciation:

- **Celebrate Achievements:** Regularly recognize and celebrate individual and team achievements.
- **Appreciation Programs:** Implement appreciation programs to reward hard work and dedication.

5. Work-Life Balance:

- **Healthy Boundaries:** Encourage employees to set healthy boundaries between work and personal life.
- **Wellness Initiatives:** Promote wellness initiatives to support physical and mental health.

6. Continuous Learning:

- **Learning Opportunities:** Provide opportunities for continuous learning and professional development.
- **Knowledge Sharing:** Encourage knowledge sharing and collaboration to enhance collective expertise.

Strategies for Building a Thriving Remote Work Culture

Implementing effective strategies can help you build and maintain a positive remote work culture. Here are some practical approaches:

1. Foster Effective Communication:

- **Communication Tools:** Use communication tools like Slack, Microsoft Teams, and Zoom to facilitate real-time communication and collaboration.
- **Regular Check-Ins:** Schedule regular check-ins and team meetings to stay connected and address any concerns.

2. Build Trust and Autonomy:

- **Goal Setting:** Set clear goals and expectations, allowing employees to take ownership of their work.
- **Supportive Leadership:** Lead by example and provide support and guidance when needed.

3. Promote Inclusivity and Diversity:

- **Diversity Initiatives:** Implement diversity initiatives to promote an inclusive work environment.
- **Employee Resource Groups:** Create employee resource groups to support diverse communities within the organization.

4. Recognize and Appreciate:

- **Recognition Programs:** Develop recognition programs that highlight and reward employees' contributions.
- **Public Acknowledgment:** Publicly acknowledge achievements through company-wide announcements or newsletters.

5. Encourage Work-Life Balance:

- **Flexible Scheduling:** Offer flexible work schedules to accommodate different time zones and personal commitments.
- **Time Off:** Encourage employees to take regular breaks and time off to recharge.

6. Support Continuous Learning:

- **Training Programs:** Provide access to training programs, courses, and workshops to support skill development.
- **Mentorship:** Establish mentorship programs to guide and support employees' professional growth.

Building Strong Team Relationships

Strong team relationships are the backbone of a thriving remote work culture. Here's how to build and nurture these relationships:

1. Virtual Team Building Activities:

- **Icebreakers:** Use icebreakers at the beginning of meetings to help team members get to know each other.
- **Social Events:** Organize virtual social events, such as online game nights or coffee breaks, to foster camaraderie.

2. Collaborative Projects:

- **Cross-Functional Teams:** Create cross-functional teams to work on projects, encouraging collaboration across different departments.
- **Brainstorming Sessions:** Hold brainstorming sessions to generate ideas and solve problems collectively.

3. Regular Feedback:

- **Constructive Feedback:** Provide regular, constructive feedback to help employees improve and grow.
- **Two-Way Communication:** Encourage employees to share their feedback and suggestions for improving team dynamics.

Leveraging Technology for Remote Work Culture

Technology plays a crucial role in building and sustaining a remote work culture. Here's how to leverage technology effectively:

1. Communication Tools:

- **Instant Messaging:** Use instant messaging tools for quick and efficient communication.
- **Video Conferencing:** Utilize video conferencing for face-to-face interactions and team meetings.

2. Project Management Tools:

- **Task Management:** Use project management tools like Trello, Asana, or Monday.com to track tasks and project progress.
- **Collaboration:** Enable team collaboration through shared documents and collaborative platforms like Google Workspace or Microsoft 365.

3. Virtual Workspaces:

- **Digital Workspaces:** Create virtual workspaces where team members can collaborate and share information.
- **Knowledge Repositories:** Develop knowledge repositories to store and share important documents and resources.

4. Employee Engagement Platforms:

- **Surveys and Polls:** Use engagement platforms to conduct surveys and polls, gathering feedback from employees.
- **Recognition Tools:** Implement recognition tools that allow peers to acknowledge and reward each other's contributions.

Measuring the Success of Your Remote Work Culture

Measuring the success of your remote work culture is essential for continuous improvement. Here are some key metrics to consider:

1. Employee Engagement:

- **Engagement Surveys:** Conduct regular engagement surveys to assess employee satisfaction and engagement levels.
- **Participation Rates:** Monitor participation rates in team activities and meetings.

2. Productivity:

- **Performance Metrics:** Track performance metrics to evaluate productivity and goal achievement.
- **Task Completion:** Measure the rate of task completion and project success.

3. Retention Rates:

- **Turnover Rates:** Monitor employee turnover rates to identify potential issues with job satisfaction.
- **Retention Initiatives:** Assess the effectiveness of retention initiatives and programs.

4. Feedback and Improvement:

- **Regular Feedback:** Collect regular feedback from employees to identify areas for improvement.
- **Continuous Improvement:** Implement changes based on feedback and continuously strive to enhance the remote work culture.

Creating a Flourishing Remote Work Culture

Building a thriving remote work culture requires dedication, effective strategies, and continuous effort. By fostering clear communication, trust, inclusivity, recognition, work-life balance, and continuous learning, you can create a positive and productive remote work environment.

Chapter 8: Leveraging Technology for Maximum Productivity

Harnessing the Power of Technology to Optimize Remote Work

In the era of remote work, technology is not just a facilitator but a vital enabler of productivity and efficiency. With the right tools and strategies, remote workers can achieve exceptional levels of performance and collaboration. This chapter delves into the various technologies that can transform your remote work experience, offering practical advice on how to leverage these tools for maximum productivity.

The Role of Technology in Remote Work

Technology bridges the gap between remote team members, enabling seamless communication, collaboration, and task management. Here's why technology is indispensable in remote work:

1. Enhances Communication:

- **Instant Connectivity:** Communication tools provide instant connectivity, making it easy to stay in touch with team members regardless of location.
- **Diverse Channels:** Various communication channels, such as video calls, instant messaging, and emails, cater to different needs and preferences.

2. Facilitates Collaboration:

- **Shared Workspaces:** Collaborative platforms allow team members to work on documents and projects simultaneously, enhancing teamwork.
- **Real-Time Updates:** Tools that offer real-time updates ensure everyone is on the same page and can track changes instantly.

3. Streamlines Task Management:

- **Task Tracking:** Project management tools help in tracking tasks, deadlines, and progress, ensuring nothing falls through the cracks.
- **Automation:** Automation tools handle repetitive tasks, freeing up time for more strategic work.

4. Boosts Productivity:

- **Focus Tools:** Productivity tools help minimize distractions and maintain focus.
- **Efficiency Apps:** Applications designed to enhance efficiency ensure optimal use of time and resources.

Essential Tools for Remote Work

To maximize productivity in a remote work setting, it's crucial to use the right tools. Here's a comprehensive list of essential tools and their functionalities:

1. Communication Tools:

- **Slack:** A versatile platform for instant messaging, file sharing, and integrating various apps.
- **Zoom:** Popular for video conferencing, webinars, and virtual meetings, offering high-quality video and audio.
- **Microsoft Teams:** Combines chat, video meetings, file storage, and app integration.

2. Project Management Tools:

- **Trello:** A visual tool for organizing tasks and projects using boards, lists, and cards.
- **Asana:** Helps teams coordinate and manage work with task assignments, timelines, and project tracking.
- **Monday.com:** A customizable work operating system for planning, tracking, and delivering team projects.

3. Collaboration Tools:

- **Google Workspace:** Offers cloud-based productivity tools like Google Docs, Sheets, and Drive for real-time collaboration.
- **Microsoft 365:** Provides a suite of applications including Word, Excel, and OneDrive for document sharing and collaboration.
- **Notion:** An all-in-one workspace for note-taking, project management, and collaboration.

4. File Sharing and Storage:

- **Dropbox:** Cloud storage for file sharing and collaboration with robust security features.
- **Box:** A secure platform for managing and sharing files and documents.
- **OneDrive:** Microsoft's cloud storage solution, integrated with Office 365.

5. Time Management Tools:

- **Toggl:** A time tracking tool that helps monitor how much time is spent on various tasks and projects.
- **RescueTime:** Tracks time spent on different applications and websites, providing insights into productivity patterns.

- **Clockify:** A time tracking and timesheet app that supports team time tracking and reporting.

6. Focus and Productivity Apps:

- **Focus@Will:** Uses music scientifically designed to improve focus and concentration.
- **Forest:** A focus app that encourages productivity by growing a virtual tree when you stay focused.
- **Pomodoro Timer:** Utilizes the Pomodoro Technique to break work into intervals with short breaks.

Best Practices for Leveraging Technology

Maximizing the benefits of technology in remote work requires thoughtful implementation and usage. Here are some best practices to consider:

1. Choose the Right Tools:

- **Needs Assessment:** Evaluate your team's specific needs and choose tools that align with those requirements.
- **User-Friendly:** Opt for tools that are user-friendly and require minimal training.

2. Ensure Seamless Integration:

- **Tool Compatibility:** Select tools that integrate seamlessly with each other to avoid siloed information.
- **API Connections:** Use API connections to automate workflows between different tools.

3. Prioritize Security:

- **Data Protection:** Ensure the tools you use have robust security features to protect sensitive data.
- **Regular Updates:** Keep software updated to protect against vulnerabilities.

4. Provide Training and Support:

- **Onboarding:** Offer comprehensive onboarding for new tools to ensure all team members are comfortable using them.
- **Ongoing Support:** Provide ongoing support and resources to help team members troubleshoot issues and maximize tool usage.

5. Establish Clear Guidelines:

- **Usage Policies:** Develop clear policies on tool usage to ensure consistency and efficiency.
- **Communication Protocols:** Define communication protocols to streamline interactions and avoid misunderstandings.

Real-Life Success Stories

Understanding how other organizations have successfully leveraged technology can provide valuable insights. Here are a few real-life success stories:

1. Automattic (WordPress):

- **Communication:** Uses Slack for instant messaging and Zoom for video calls to maintain constant communication.

- **Collaboration:** Employs P2, a custom WordPress theme, for asynchronous communication and project updates.
- **Success:** Automattic has thrived as a fully remote company, with a strong emphasis on transparency and collaboration.

2. Buffer:

- **Transparency:** Uses tools like Slack and Discourse for open communication and transparency across the organization.
- **Project Management:** Relies on Trello for managing projects and tracking progress.
- **Success:** Buffer's remote culture is built on trust and transparency, leading to high employee satisfaction and productivity.

3. Zapier:

- **Automation:** Utilizes its own platform to automate workflows and integrate various tools.
- **Documentation:** Maintains comprehensive documentation in Notion for knowledge sharing and onboarding.
- **Success:** Zapier's efficient use of automation and clear documentation has enabled it to operate smoothly as a remote-first company.

Overcoming Challenges in Technology Adoption

Adopting new technology comes with its challenges. Here's how to overcome common hurdles:

1. Resistance to Change:

- **Involve Employees:** Involve employees in the selection process to increase buy-in and reduce resistance.

- **Training:** Provide thorough training to ease the transition and build confidence in using new tools.

2. Technical Issues:

- **Support Systems:** Establish robust support systems to address technical issues promptly.
- **Regular Maintenance:** Perform regular maintenance and updates to ensure smooth operation.

3. Information Overload:

- **Streamline Tools:** Avoid using too many tools that can overwhelm employees. Choose a few that meet most needs.
- **Centralized Information:** Use centralized platforms for storing and accessing information to reduce confusion.

4. Security Concerns:

- **Encryption:** Ensure all tools use encryption for data protection.
- **Access Controls:** Implement access controls to restrict sensitive information to authorized personnel only.

Future Trends in Remote Work Technology

The landscape of remote work technology is constantly evolving. Here are some future trends to watch:

1. Artificial Intelligence (AI) and Automation:

- **AI Assistants:** AI-powered virtual assistants will become more prevalent, helping with task management and customer support.

- **Automated Workflows:** Increased use of automation to handle repetitive tasks and improve efficiency.

2. Virtual and Augmented Reality (VR/AR):

- **Virtual Meetings:** VR and AR will revolutionize virtual meetings, making them more immersive and interactive.
- **Training and Onboarding:** VR/AR can enhance training and onboarding experiences by providing realistic simulations.

3. Enhanced Collaboration Tools:

- **Real-Time Collaboration:** Tools with enhanced real-time collaboration features will continue to emerge, improving team interactions.
- **Integrated Platforms:** More integrated platforms that combine multiple functionalities into a single interface.

4. Cybersecurity Advances:

- **Advanced Protection:** As cyber threats evolve, advanced cybersecurity measures will become essential for protecting remote work environments.
- **Zero Trust Models:** Adoption of Zero Trust security models to ensure continuous verification of users and devices.

Empowering Remote Work Through Technology

Technology is the cornerstone of a successful remote work strategy. By leveraging the right tools and best practices, remote teams can achieve high productivity levels, collaboration, and satisfaction.

Chapter 9: Practical Tips for Creating a Productive Remote Work Environment

Optimizing Your Remote Work Setup for Maximum Efficiency

Creating a productive remote work environment is crucial for maintaining focus, efficiency, and overall well-being. With the right strategies, you can transform your home or any remote location into a powerhouse of productivity. This chapter offers practical tips and insights to help you set up and maintain an optimal remote work environment.

The Importance of a Well-Designed Work Environment

A well-designed work environment can significantly impact your productivity and mental health. Here's why it matters:

1. Enhances Focus:

- **Dedicated Workspace:** A designated workspace helps separate work from personal life, enhancing concentration.
- **Minimal Distractions:** An organized and quiet space minimizes distractions, allowing for deep focus.

2. Boosts Efficiency:

- **Ergonomic Setup:** Proper ergonomics prevent discomfort and physical strain, enabling longer and more comfortable work sessions.

- **Efficient Tools:** Access to the right tools and resources streamlines tasks and reduces time wastage.

3. **Supports Well-Being:**

    - **Mental Health:** A pleasant and comfortable environment reduces stress and promotes mental well-being.
    - **Work-Life Balance:** Clear boundaries between work and personal life help maintain a healthy work-life balance.

Setting Up Your Remote Workspace

Designing an effective remote workspace involves several key considerations:

1. **Choosing the Right Location:**

    - **Quiet Area:** Select a quiet area in your home or remote location where you can work without interruptions.
    - **Natural Light:** Ensure your workspace has access to natural light, which boosts mood and energy levels.

2. **Ergonomic Furniture:**

    - **Comfortable Chair:** Invest in a high-quality, ergonomic chair that provides proper support for your back and posture.
    - **Adjustable Desk:** Use an adjustable desk that allows you to alternate between sitting and standing, promoting better circulation and reducing fatigue.

3. **Essential Equipment:**

- **Reliable Computer:** Ensure you have a reliable computer or laptop with the necessary specifications to handle your work tasks efficiently.
- **High-Speed Internet:** A stable and high-speed internet connection is vital for seamless communication and access to online resources.

4. Proper Lighting:

- **Task Lighting:** Use task lighting to illuminate your workspace adequately, reducing eye strain.
- **Ambient Lighting:** Soft ambient lighting creates a comfortable atmosphere without causing glare on screens.

5. Organization and Storage:

- **Declutter:** Keep your workspace clutter-free to maintain focus and reduce stress.
- **Storage Solutions:** Use storage solutions like shelves, drawers, and organizers to keep essential items within reach and maintain order.

6. Personal Touches:

- **Inspiring Decor:** Add personal touches such as artwork, plants, or motivational quotes to make your workspace inspiring and enjoyable.
- **Comfort Items:** Include comfort items like a cozy blanket or cushion to enhance your comfort during long work hours.

Productivity Tips and Techniques

Implementing effective productivity techniques can further enhance your remote work environment:

1. Time Management:

- **Pomodoro Technique:** Use the Pomodoro Technique to work in focused intervals with short breaks, maintaining high levels of concentration.
- **Time Blocking:** Schedule specific blocks of time for different tasks to structure your day and ensure you allocate time for all priorities.

2. Task Prioritization:

- **Eisenhower Matrix:** Use the Eisenhower Matrix to categorize tasks by urgency and importance, helping you focus on what matters most.
- **Daily To-Do List:** Create a daily to-do list with clear, actionable tasks to stay organized and on track.

3. Minimizing Distractions:

- **Do Not Disturb Mode:** Use the do not disturb mode on your devices to minimize interruptions from notifications and calls.
- **Focused Work Sessions:** Set specific times for focused work sessions where you eliminate distractions and dedicate your attention to critical tasks.

4. Regular Breaks:

- **Microbreaks:** Take short microbreaks every hour to stretch, hydrate, and refresh your mind.
- **Lunchtime Breaks:** Ensure you take a proper lunch break away from your workspace to recharge and avoid burnout.

5. Efficient Communication:

- **Clear Guidelines:** Establish clear communication guidelines with your team to ensure efficient and effective exchanges.
- **Regular Check-Ins:** Schedule regular check-ins with your team or manager to stay aligned and address any challenges promptly.

6. Leveraging Technology:

- **Productivity Apps:** Utilize productivity apps and tools to manage tasks, track time, and stay organized.
- **Automation Tools:** Use automation tools to handle repetitive tasks and streamline workflows, freeing up time for more strategic work.

Maintaining Work-Life Balance

Balancing work and personal life is essential for long-term productivity and well-being:

1. Set Boundaries:

- **Defined Work Hours:** Establish clear work hours and stick to them, avoiding the temptation to work beyond your scheduled time.
- **Personal Time:** Allocate specific times for personal activities, hobbies, and relaxation to ensure you recharge and maintain a healthy balance.

2. Create a Routine:

- **Morning Routine:** Develop a morning routine that prepares you mentally and physically for the workday ahead.
- **Evening Routine:** Implement an evening routine to wind down and transition from work mode to personal time.

3. **Stay Connected:**

- **Social Interaction:** Make time for social interactions with friends, family, and colleagues to maintain connections and support networks.
- **Virtual Events:** Participate in virtual events, webinars, and social activities to stay engaged and combat feelings of isolation.

4. **Physical Activity:**

- **Exercise:** Incorporate regular physical activity into your routine to boost energy levels and reduce stress.
- **Stretching:** Perform stretching exercises throughout the day to alleviate tension and improve circulation.

Overcoming Common Remote Work Challenges

Remote work presents unique challenges that can impact productivity. Here's how to overcome them:

1. **Isolation:**

- **Virtual Collaboration:** Engage in virtual collaboration and team-building activities to foster a sense of community.
- **Support Groups:** Join remote work support groups or communities to share experiences and gain insights.

2. **Procrastination:**

- **Set Goals:** Set clear, achievable goals and deadlines to stay motivated and focused.

- **Accountability Partner:** Partner with a colleague or friend to hold each other accountable for meeting deadlines and staying productive.

3. Burnout:

- **Recognize Signs:** Be aware of the signs of burnout, such as exhaustion, irritability, and decreased performance.
- **Self-Care:** Prioritize self-care activities like meditation, hobbies, and relaxation techniques to prevent burnout.

4. Distractions:

- **Dedicated Workspace:** Ensure your workspace is separate from high-traffic areas and distractions.
- **Noise-Canceling Headphones:** Use noise-canceling headphones to block out background noise and maintain focus.

Real-Life Examples of Productive Remote Work Setups

Learning from successful remote work setups can provide inspiration and practical insights. Here are a few examples:

1. Tech Entrepreneur:

- **Ergonomic Setup:** A tech entrepreneur uses an ergonomic chair and standing desk to maintain comfort and productivity.
- **Smart Home Office:** Incorporates smart home devices like voice-activated assistants and automated lighting to enhance efficiency.

2. Freelance Writer:

- **Inspiring Environment:** A freelance writer decorates their workspace with motivational quotes, plants, and personal mementos.
- **Productivity Tools:** Utilizes productivity tools like Trello for task management and Grammarly for writing assistance.

3. Remote Project Manager:

- **Collaboration Platforms:** A remote project manager relies on collaboration platforms like Asana and Slack to coordinate with their team.
- **Time Management:** Implements time management techniques like time blocking and the Pomodoro Technique to stay on track.

Optimizing Your Remote Work Environment for Success

Creating a productive remote work environment requires thoughtful planning, the right tools, and effective strategies. By optimizing your workspace, implementing productivity techniques, and maintaining work-life balance, you can achieve exceptional levels of efficiency and well-being.

Chapter 10: Strategies for Maintaining Work-Life Balance

Achieving Harmony Between Professional and Personal Life

In the era of remote work, maintaining a healthy work-life balance is essential for long-term productivity, mental well-being, and overall satisfaction. The lines between work and personal life can easily blur when your home becomes your office, making it crucial to adopt strategies that help you achieve harmony between the two. This chapter provides detailed insights and practical tips to help you balance your professional and personal life effectively.

The Importance of Work-Life Balance

Work-life balance is not just about allocating equal time to work and personal activities; it's about ensuring that neither aspect dominates your life to the detriment of the other. Here's why it matters:

1. Enhances Productivity:

- **Sustained Energy:** A balanced life ensures you have the energy and focus needed to be productive at work.
- **Avoids Burnout:** Regular breaks and personal time prevent burnout, enabling you to perform consistently well.

2. Improves Mental Health:

- **Reduces Stress:** Balancing work and personal life reduces stress and anxiety, contributing to better mental health.
- **Promotes Happiness:** Engaging in personal activities and hobbies enhances happiness and life satisfaction.

3. Strengthens Relationships:

- **Quality Time:** Spending quality time with family and friends strengthens relationships and support networks.
- **Work-Life Harmony:** Achieving harmony between work and personal life fosters a sense of fulfillment and well-being.

Setting Boundaries Between Work and Personal Life

Establishing clear boundaries is crucial for maintaining work-life balance. Here's how to do it effectively:

1. Define Work Hours:

- **Consistent Schedule:** Set a consistent work schedule that defines your start and end times.
- **Communicate Boundaries:** Inform your colleagues and family members of your work hours to minimize interruptions.

2. Create a Dedicated Workspace:

- **Separate Space:** Designate a specific area in your home for work, separate from personal spaces.
- **Workspace Rules:** Establish rules for your workspace, such as no personal activities during work hours.

3. Take Regular Breaks:

- **Scheduled Breaks:** Schedule regular breaks throughout the day to rest and recharge.
- **Physical Activity:** Use breaks to engage in physical activity, such as stretching or walking, to boost energy levels.

4. Disconnect After Work:

- **Log Off:** Log off from work-related apps and emails at the end of your workday.
- **Unplug:** Avoid checking work messages during personal time to fully disconnect and relax.

Effective Time Management Techniques

Managing your time effectively is key to balancing work and personal life. Here are some proven techniques:

1. Prioritize Tasks:

- **Urgent vs. Important:** Use the Eisenhower Matrix to prioritize tasks based on urgency and importance.
- **Daily Goals:** Set daily goals and focus on completing high-priority tasks first.

2. Time Blocking:

- **Structured Schedule:** Allocate specific blocks of time for different tasks and activities.
- **Focus Sessions:** Use time blocks for focused work sessions, followed by breaks.

3. The Pomodoro Technique:

- **Work Intervals:** Work in intervals of 25 minutes, followed by a 5-minute break.
- **Long Breaks:** After four intervals, take a longer break of 15-30 minutes to recharge.

4. Delegate and Automate:

- **Delegate Tasks:** Delegate tasks to colleagues or family members to lighten your workload.
- **Automation Tools:** Use automation tools to handle repetitive tasks and streamline workflows.

Incorporating Self-Care into Your Routine

Self-care is essential for maintaining balance and well-being. Here's how to incorporate it into your routine:

1. Physical Health:

- **Regular Exercise:** Engage in regular physical exercise to boost energy and reduce stress.
- **Healthy Diet:** Maintain a balanced diet to fuel your body and mind.

2. Mental Health:

- **Mindfulness Practices:** Practice mindfulness techniques, such as meditation or deep breathing, to calm your mind.
- **Therapy and Counseling:** Seek professional support if needed to address mental health concerns.

3. Personal Interests and Hobbies:

- **Pursue Hobbies:** Make time for hobbies and activities that you enjoy and that relax you.

- **Creative Outlets:** Engage in creative activities, such as painting or writing, to express yourself and unwind.

4. Social Connections:

- **Stay Connected:** Maintain regular contact with friends and family through calls, video chats, or in-person visits.
- **Join Communities:** Participate in social or professional communities to build connections and support networks.

Balancing Family and Work Responsibilities

Balancing family responsibilities with work can be challenging but achievable with the right strategies:

1. Establish a Routine:

- **Consistent Routine:** Establish a daily routine that includes work, family time, and personal activities.
- **Flexible Schedule:** Be flexible with your schedule to accommodate family needs and responsibilities.

2. Share Responsibilities:

- **Family Involvement:** Involve family members in household tasks and responsibilities.
- **Task Sharing:** Share tasks with your partner or children to lighten the load and foster teamwork.

3. Quality Time:

- **Dedicated Time:** Dedicate specific times for family activities and ensure you are fully present.
- **Meaningful Activities:** Engage in meaningful activities with your family, such as game nights or outdoor adventures.

4. Communicate Openly:

- **Clear Communication:** Communicate openly with your family about your work schedule and any challenges.
- **Set Expectations:** Set clear expectations for work and family time to avoid misunderstandings.

Adapting to Changing Circumstances

Life is dynamic, and circumstances can change unexpectedly. Here's how to adapt while maintaining balance:

1. Flexibility:

- **Be Adaptable:** Be open to adjusting your schedule and routines as needed to accommodate changes.
- **Plan Ahead:** Anticipate potential changes and plan ahead to minimize disruptions.

2. Resilience:

- **Stay Positive:** Maintain a positive outlook and focus on finding solutions to challenges.
- **Learn from Setbacks:** Use setbacks as opportunities to learn and grow, building resilience.

3. Support Systems:

- **Seek Support:** Reach out to friends, family, or professional networks for support during challenging times.
- **Offer Support:** Be willing to offer support to others, fostering a sense of community and mutual aid.

4. Continuous Improvement:

- **Reflect Regularly:** Regularly reflect on your work-life balance and make adjustments as needed.
- **Set New Goals:** Set new goals and priorities based on your evolving needs and circumstances.

Real-Life Examples of Work-Life Balance

Learning from real-life examples can provide valuable insights and inspiration. Here are a few stories:

1. The Entrepreneur:

- **Routine and Flexibility:** An entrepreneur balances work and personal life by establishing a routine that includes dedicated work hours and family time.
- **Self-Care:** Prioritizes self-care activities such as exercise and mindfulness to maintain well-being and productivity.

2. The Remote Employee:

- **Clear Boundaries:** A remote employee sets clear boundaries by having a dedicated workspace and defined work hours.
- **Time Management:** Uses time management techniques like time blocking and the Pomodoro Technique to stay organized and efficient.

3. The Freelancer:

- **Task Prioritization:** A freelancer prioritizes tasks based on urgency and importance, ensuring high-priority work is completed first.

- **Work-Life Integration:** Integrates work and personal life by scheduling breaks and personal activities throughout the day.

Achieving Work-Life Balance for Long-Term Success

Maintaining work-life balance is a continuous process that requires conscious effort and regular adjustments. By setting boundaries, managing time effectively, incorporating self-care, balancing family responsibilities, and adapting to changing circumstances, you can achieve a harmonious and fulfilling life.

www.ingramcontent.com/pod-product-compliance
Lightning Source LLC
Chambersburg PA
CBHW071953210526
45479CB00003B/919